Fu STORIES & JOKES
for Speakers

Funny STORIES & JOKES
for Speakers

Compiled by
Geoffrey Matson

foulsham

LONDON · NEW YORK · TORONTO · SYDNEY

foulsham

Yeovil Road, Slough, Berkshire SL1 4JH

ISBN 0-572-01615-8

Copyright © 1990 W. Foulsham and Co. Ltd
Originally published as *Stories For Speakers*

Printed in Great Britain by
St Edmundsbury Press Ltd
Bury St Edmunds, Suffolk

Contents

Not the Answer he Expected

I always think the following is a rather clever story and it is very useful for including in a speech at some function which is attended by such persons as scientists or men with business interests.

A number of people were being shown a new and exciting computer which could work out any calculation instantly, and which also, it was claimed, could give an accurate answer to any sort of question.

One member of the party suggested that a question should be fed into it to test its ability. He typed on a piece of paper: 'What is my father doing now?' The question was fed in at one end of the machine, and almost immediately a typed reply came out at the other end which read: 'Your father is driving off at the first tee at St Andrews'.

'This is utterly ridiculous,' said the person who had asked the question, 'the machine has definitely slipped up here; my father has been dead for more than ten years.'

'Why not feed this information into the machine and see what sort of reply it gives you?' said another member of the party.

This was done, and almost immediately, as before, the reply came out at the other end, saying: 'You are mistaken. Your mother's *husband* died more than ten years ago; your *father* is now putting on the second green at St Andrews.'

Lord Boothby, K.B.E., Ll.D.

Good Company

I do a great deal of public speaking which (not being a nice or modest person) I thoroughly enjoy: but one can be mauled by Chairmen.

For example, at a small Welsh Literary and Philosophic Society I was greeted by a Madam Chairman, and an audience of Welsh literary and philosophic types, who obviously couldn't imagine why *I* was there. Madam Chairman, recognizing the looks of corporate dismay with which my presence had been greeted, told the audience that I was there because I was an author.

The look of dismay changed to one of rude and frank incredulity.

So then she told them the titles of all the books I'd written, and how beautifully each was written (in my opinion, perfectly true!), but *still* the audience looked rudely incredulous.

So, in a last desperate attempt to establish my right to stand up and talk to the intelligentsia of South East Wales, Madam Chairman said firmly: 'Indeed, ladies and gentlemen, I *myself* have spent many pleasant nights in *bed* with Mr Braddon!'

Russell Braddon

Christmas Dinner

The following is a useful story worth telling at almost any kind of function around Christmas time.

Two natives were sitting chatting out in the forest, beside their cauldron, when one suddenly asked, 'What are we going to have for our Christmas dinner this year?'

'That's easy,' said the other, 'we'll start a revolution.'

'Start a revolution?' said his friend. 'How on earth is that going to help?'

'Well,' said the other, 'if we start a revolution the U.N. will quickly send over an observer, and then we can eat *him*!'

Harry Secombe, C.B.E.

He missed his Cap

This is a story which appeals to me and which can easily be fitted into a speech made at numerous, and varied functions.

A young constable who was fresh to the Force was sent for duty to a provincial town and interviewed by the Superintendent. 'Now, young man,' said the latter, 'I understand you are anxious to get on. I want you to look into the after-hours drinking at the "Haunch of Venison". We've given the landlord several warnings, but he just goes on ignoring them. I want you to go home, change into civvies, and then go into the bar and see if he'll serve you after time has been called. If he does, *do* him. He's had it coming for a long time.'

Anxious to please, the young copper went home, put on his sports jacket and flannel trousers and went off to the "Haunch of Venison". He had a pint or two, and just as the landlord shouted 'Time, Gentlemen, please: Houses of Parliament, gentlemen, *please!*' he put his tankard forward and asked for a re-fill.

'Didn't you hear me call "time"?' said the landlord. 'Well,' said the young constable, 'it'll do no harm; I'll have drunk it in a couple of ticks; go on!'

'What,' exclaimed the landlord, 'make me look a right ninny for serving a copper after hours?'

Taken aback, the young constable asked, 'But how do you know I *am* a copper?'

'Blimey,' replied the landlord, 'you've still got your helmet on!'

Franklin Engelmann

10

Obvious Mistake

As a clergyman, I have often found the following story worth telling.

It concerns a number of fellows who were having to suffer a severe bombardment in Flanders in the First World War. Shells were coming over thick and fast, and they were all getting very worried.

At length, one of them said: 'Let's do something: let's pray.' They offered a prayer but still the shells continued to fall around them unhindered. 'That doesn't seem to be much use,' said one.' Let's sing a hymn.' So they sang a hymn, but the bombardment went ominously on.

Finally, one of them piped up cheerfully, 'You know what's wrong?'

'No,' said the others eagerly, 'what?'

'Well,' said the one with the bright idea, 'we haven't taken up the collection yet!'

Rev John Phillips

Fame at Last

I have told this story at my expense in an after dinner speech at a function in my honour.

Some time ago I received a postcard addressed to 'Mr Shinwell, England'. Imagine: Mr Shinwell, England. At last I had arrived. The postal authorities, of course, delivered it to me, so don't think this is the first time I have been honoured. However, being of an inquisitive turn of mind, I looked at what was written on the other side. And what do you think it said? In five words of boldly written letters, it merely said: 'Shut up you big mouth!'

*   *   *

When Ramsay Macdonald was Prime Minister, a colleague of mine, Mr Rhys Davies, M.P., went to America to lecture. In one small township, the chairman introduced Mr Davies in the following fashion. 'By all accounts over in England, they have what is called a Prime Minister, and our speaker tonight is his right-hand man.'

After the meeting, my colleague accompanied the chairman to the ante-room to settle up. Davies said to the chairman: 'It was kind of you to describe me as Macdonald's right-hand man, but really I am only an ordinary member of Parliament.'

'Don't worry,' said the chairman, 'before you arrived nobody had ever heard of you, and after you have gone, everybody will have forgotten you; sign on the dotted line!'

Emanuel Shinwell, M.P.

Tit for Tat

The following story is particularly appropriate for telling at some function where magicians are present, but it can easily be worked into speeches made on other occasions.

A famous magician went to a small country in the far East, full of mystery and charm, and was asked if he would give a special show in the Sultan's Palace. The Sultan and his family were all intensely interested in magic.

The magician agreed, and put on a really spectacular show, finishing with a trick for which he required a ring from a member of his audience. At the time, the Sultan's daughter was wearing a beautiful one set with a large pearl. The magician asked if he could borrow it and she took it from her finger and gave it to him. He promptly threw it through a window, and at the same moment a dove flew in through a window on the opposite side of the room, and fluttered on to the magician's shoulder.

It had a ribbon round its neck, and hanging from the ribbon was a ring. The magician cut the ribbon, took off the ring, and handed back to the Sultan's daughter the actual ring he had just borrowed. She took it, placed it back on her finger, and then plunged her hand and arm deep down into her corsage, and producing a magnificent double bed and chest of drawers she handed them to the magician in appreciation of his performance.

David Nixon

The Musical Lions

Having Lenny the Lion as my constant companion, I am naturally interested in any story dealing with lions. For example, here is one which I find funny.

The violinist was bragging that he could tame any wild animal simply by playing his violin. He was willing to wager £100 to win his point. His offer was taken up by a circus lion-tamer who said that if the musician could tame *his* three lions, he would be happy to lose £100.

The violinist duly took up his position in the circus ring, started to play his own brand of sweet music and shouted, 'Right, let the first lion in.' Leo came bounding into the ring, but as soon as he heard the music, he assumed a dreamy expression, curled up on the floor and listened intently. 'Right,' shouted the violinist, 'let the second lion in.' Leo number two came racing into the ring but stopped short as soon as he heard the romantic music. He too, curled up and listened absolutely enthralled.

The violinist then called for the third lion to be let in. This one bounded into the ring, made straight for the violinist and ate him up! The other two lions turned to lion number three and said, 'What did you have to go and do that for when we were listening to such beautiful music?' The third lion merely cupped his paw to his ear and said, 'Eh?'

Terry (Lenny the Lion) Hall

Not the Right Cooking

Here is a little story which can be included in an after-dinner speech of almost any kind.

Two cannibals were conversing together, and one of them was complaining to the other of a very bad stomach-ache that he had.

His friend asked what he had been eating, and he said, 'Oh, the usual thing. I got a very nice Missionary the other day, and he was very tasty indeed; I enjoyed him. But I seem to have had an awful pain ever since.'

His friend said, 'But what sort of a Missionary was he? How was he dressed?'

He said, 'He had a very long brown sort of coat on, which went down to the floor, and a rope round his waist.'

His friend said, 'How did you cook him?'

He said, 'Oh, the usual way. I put him in a cauldron and boiled him up.'

His friend said, 'Oh, but that was your mistake. You should not have boiled him. You see, *he was a Friar*!'

Sir Malcolm Sargent

An Awkward Moment

The following personal experience has been worth re-telling on more than one occasion.

I was compering a concert in a Mental Hospital several years ago, and for one little 'gimmick' wore a pyjama jacket. I had announced an act which I knew would take at least fifteen minutes, slipped the pyjama jacket on, and took a walk along a couple of corridors, just to pass the time. A man in uniform came up to me and said, 'And what are you supposed to be doing?' I said, 'Oh just wandering around.' He said, 'Oh yes, and who are you?' I said, 'I'm Sandy Sandford.' He said, Yes, and I'm Kenneth Horne. Get back to bed!' It took me about ten minutes to convince this man that I was compering the show!

Sandy Sandford

Interesting Dreams

This story is one I have made up myself, and it seems to go down very well whenever it is told.

A husband and wife were talking one morning, and the wife was telling the husband about a very unusual dream she had during the night. In her dream she said that she saw herself at a rather unusual auction where they were selling male muscles. She said you could get a beautiful set of back muscles, just right for gardening, for £40; a set of chest muscles, ideal for a girl to lean her head on, for £50; and a wonderful set of arm muscles, ideal for cuddling, for £60.

'Did you see any muscles like mine?' asked the husband. 'Yes, they were selling that sort in bundles of a dozen for a shilling.'

The next morning, the husband told his wife that he, too, had dreamed about an auction. He explained that, in his dream, they were selling women's mouths. He explained that you could buy a mouth with a pretty pursed-up pair of lips for £50; a mouth with a pair of lips attractively pink like a rose, for £60; and a mouth with a sexy pair of Spanish lips for £100.

'Did you see a mouth like mine?' asked his wife eagerly.

'Yes,' replied her husband, *they were holding the auction in that.*

Cardew Robinson

A Typical Winstonian Description

Sir Winston Churchill and Lady Violet Bonham Carter, many years ago, found themselves sitting next to each other at a private dance. At the next door table were some young noisy people including two young ladies who had recently figured in spectacular divorce cases.

Lady Violet remarked upon this to Sir Winston and added that their parents would not have had two such young ladies in their houses. 'They are stained, Winston,' she said, 'stained.'

Sir Winston was a little taken aback at the vehemence of the word stained, but replied, 'Stained, Violet? Possibly. Stained but positive. How unlike those flaccid amoebae of virtue who can barely wiggle their antennae in the turgid water of negativity.'

*   *   *

Another Winston story is this. When I was Under-Secretary at the Home Office, I wanted to spend the Easter holiday with my brother-in-law who lives in County Mayo in Southern Ireland. All ministers, however junior, have to obtain the Prime Minister's permission to leave the country and I accordingly asked the Home Secretary, then the Hon. William Lloyd George, to approach Sir Winston.

Unfortunately a flare up on the Ulster/Eire border including several shootings and the burning of a police station, broke out shortly after I had made my application. Sir Winston at first seemed reluctant to let me go but on being assured by the Home Secretary that my visit was purely social, and I should not be making any political speeches or taking part in public affairs, (the Home Office is constitutionally responsible to Parliament for Ulster affairs), he observed, 'Very well then, he may go, but *he must participate in no uprisings.*'

*   *   *

Lastly—a speaker addressing a Welsh audience was carried away with the Welsh enthusiasm and spiritual fire which the Welsh call Huwyl, and on resuming his seat he apologised to his chairman for having exceeded by a long way the time allocated to him for his speech.

'No, not at all,' said the chairman reassuringly, 'that was not too long at all. You have merely shortened the winter for us.'

Lord Mancroft, K.B.E.

An Awkward Situation

In 1961 the English Legal Profession went to America for a conference with the American Bar Association.

On the occasion when the American Bar Association gave a dinner to the 1,500 visiting English lawyers, about 3,500 people sat down to a champagne dinner. It was expected that the speaker in chief would be Mr Adlai Stevenson. Unfortunately, however, at the time he was in bed with an injured knee and his place was taken by Mr Richard Nixon, who started his address by stating that this situation reminded him of a story he had heard some years ago from England.

The story concerned an elderly Vicar living in a very remote Parish, who was terribly upset at the sudden demise of his wife who had been his constant companion over the years, and who played the organ at all his services.

The Vicar did not know where to turn to find another organist, so in desperation, he sent a telegram to his Bishop which read as follows—'Most urgent—my wife is dead—please send substitute for week-end.'

Mr Nixon remarked that he was indeed a substitute for Mr Stevenson, but he did not play the organ.

R. A. Copley

Looking for an Audience

You know, elections are a tame business now compared with the old days, and I should think a little research into some of the 19th century campaigns would be well worth while. The trouble with modern elections is that the result is generally a foregone conclusion, and the age of huge political rallies died anyway with the advent of television. The other day I was dining in the House of Commons with Scholefield Allen, Member for Crewe, and Donald Wade, Huddersfield West, and the conversation turned to by-election meetings. Mr Scholefield Allen described an occasion when he and the local Chairman had turned up at the hall at the announced time, to find not a single soul there. They decided to wait at the door and greet the audience as they arrived, but after half an hour, the place was still deserted and the two hopefuls were getting rather chilly. They had given up, and were disconsolately wandering back into the hall to warm up by the fire, when Scholefield Allen noticed that after all, there was one elderly lady sitting patiently in the gloom near the door. Delighted to see such a faithful supporter, they fell upon her with a long exposition of the Party's excellent prospects in the by-election, and the current state of the nation. Finally, the silent lady got her chance to intervene. 'I'm the caretaker,' she said, 'can I lock up now?'

Donald Wade then recounted a similar experience of his own. In his story the lone attender was a young man of obvious intelligence and capability, who would be, Donald thought, a great asset to the local organisation in their campaign and, moreover, had sound Liberal views as the conversation showed. Donald told the young man how glad he was that he had come along to the meeting. 'I thought I'd better,' was the reply, 'considering I'm the candidate!'

*   *   *

Of all my own experiences at political meetings, my favourite has been to listen to my friend Dominic Le Foe dealing with hecklers. He always seems to attract them, and is absolutely devastating on every occasion. At the West Bromwich by-election last year, we had a vocal Labour supporter in the audience, who kept interrupting Dominic's remarks about the Profumo affair with ancient examples of improper behaviour by Liberal politicians. 'What about Lloyd George and the Marconi scandal of 1911?' he shouted several times. Finally Dominic stopped in the middle of a sentence and turned on the historian. 'You'll get a shock when you visit the cinema again,' he said, 'you'll find they've taken the piano away!'

Eric Lubbock, M.P.

Not what I Expected

I was invited to speak at a luncheon on the occasion of a small agricultural and flower show.

I was wondering what theme to use as the rain was teeming down on the marquee roof, when I decided to point out the average housewife's absolute refusal to recognize value for money.

'Why,' I asked 'should they grumble about milk at 35p per pint, while lemonade, which is only CO_2 and H_2O cost more than 80p.'

The audience were convulsed with mirth, so much so, that I asked the President of the Show who sat next to me, why they were so amused.

He said, 'Well, I happen to be the proprietor of this town's Mineral Water Factory!'

*   *   *

The following story will appeal to most countrymen, but may not make much sense to the average townsman.

A certain farmer had a long standing ambition to win a first prize at the Royal Show with a ram lamb. At last he thought that he had detected a potential winner amongst his flock. With great enthusiasm he brought this animal up with meticulous food and care.

When the Royal show was over he was disappointed not to be in the money at all. 'Never mind,' he thought, 'it should do well at the County Show.' Again the same story—not a place. Hopes dashed, the farmer decided to enter the lamb for the Village Show, where he was mortified to see his sheep at the bottom of the class.

He took the ram home, put him in a pen, and deep in thought, surveyed the subject of his lost hopes.

Just then his neighbour walked by.

'Lovely weather, George,' he cried.

'He will be tomorrow,' said the farmer.

(For the benefit of the uninitiated, a wether' is a castrated sheep.)

Ted Moult

Please Step Aside

When I was a law student we held a dinner of Gray's Inn men. The chair was taken by Trevor Watson, (later a well-known K.C.) who was a minute man in size. Our guest was Gilbert Chesterton, a giant in height and depth. When preparing to take a photograph, the photographer in all innocence called out: 'Mr Chairman, please step aside, you are obscuring Mr Chesterton.'

Claud Mullins

Some Agricultural Stories

I have a feeling that you have to live in East Anglia to appreciate the Norfolkman's sense of humour, and I can think of many incidents which illustrate what I mean.

A story which I have often told in an after-dinner speech in East Anglia, concerns two farm workers who were drilling a field of wheat next to a straight stretch of road between Newmarket and Norwich. The field finished, they drove the outfit out of the field and on to the main road when, unfortunately, the tractor stalled right across the path of an oncoming sports car doing 90 miles an hour. The driver of the car slammed on his brakes with the result that the car slewed round in the road and burst through the hedge into the newly drilled field of wheat. The man standing on the drill watched the incident with amazement and shouted to his mate on the tractor, 'Cor blast—it's a good job we'd finished that field o' wheat—we might've been killed.'

Most countrymen have a sense of humour. I spent several months recently looking at farming in Australia, and one of the many stories I was told was about a 'pommy" who rang up the leader of a shearing gang to ask if he would shear his sheep. 'O.K. mate,' said the Australian, 'how many have you got?' 'Thirty,' said the "pommy", and as quick as lightning the shearer said, 'Can I have their names, mate?'

But the best story of all concerns a young jackeroo who found that during the first month he worked on an Australian property he was given either bacon, sausage or pork for every meal. Coming in from the fields on a hot, dusty day, he asked for a mug of cold water. He thanked his employer and said how cool and refreshing it was. 'It ought to be,' was the reply, 'it's bore water.' 'Gee,' said the jackeroo, 'you waste nothing here, do you?'

Gordon Mosley

So very Shy

It probably sounds better spoken than when written down, but I once heard an after-dinner speaker begin his remarks be saying that speaking to such a distinguished audience made him feel more shy than usual. Shyness was, as a matter of fact, a family characteristic, and it is extremely likely that had his parents not been so shy, he would be a few years older.

A story that is suitable for the last speaker on a toast list, is this one about a dog.

The speaker says something like: 'Having listened to the several speeches that have already been made this evening, I feel like a dog that has just gone down a street full of lamp posts—short of material and with hardly a leg to stand on.'

I am afraid both these anecdotes are strictly for 'men only' audiences, but they are always good for a laugh on such occasions.

Sir Miles Thomas

His Flashy, Toothy Smile

An after-dinner story that stays with me was made by Shelley Berman at a show business supper in Hollywood.

It concerns a star glamour boy actor who was making a big play for a beautiful young actress. On their first date, he decided to play it like a gentleman—took her to supper, and drove her to her home with no amorous advance except a goodnight peck, and liberal doses of his flashy, toothy smile. It wasn't until he got home that he smiled smugly at the mirror and discovered that the meal had left him with a large revolting leaf of spinach wedged prominently between his front teeth. . . .

Joe (Mr Piano) Henderson

The Son was Alright

As the Managing Director of a firm which is constantly working on various Government contracts, I am frequently in the company of Civil Servants, either in connection with business or at some social gathering. At one such gathering as the latter, some time ago, I remember a speaker telling the following story against his profession.

A man and his wife were coming up to their silver wedding anniversary and, feeling a bit nostalgic, the husband suggested it would be a good idea to pay a return visit to the church—some miles away from where they now lived—where they were married.

This they did, and on entering the church, they met the vicar, who was different from the one who had married them. The husband explained what they were doing, and mentioned the date when they were married there nearly twenty-five years ago.

The vicar thought for a minute and then said, 'I think there were certain irregularities about this time in the keeping of the records and, although I hate to tell you this, it may be that you are not legally married. If you wait a minute, I will go into the vestry and have a look.'

After a few minutes he returned, looking rather solemn, and said, Yes, it is as I thought, it was at the time of your wedding that the irregularity took place, and actually you were not properly married.'

'Does that mean then, that I am still a bachelor?' asked the husband.

'Yes, I'm afraid it does.'

'I suppose then, I am still legally a spinster?' said the wife.

'I am sorry, but I suppose it does.'

Their teenage son, who was with them, had heard all this, and he turned to his father rather blankly and asked, 'Well, Dad, what does all this make me?'

'You're alright,' said his father quickly, 'I've got *you* entered for the Civil Service.

Company Director

Some Helpful Friends

Maybe the best thing I can do is to tell you of some of the people who wrote to me during my long struggle to renounce my title so that I could remain in the House of Commons.

The following is part of a speech I made in Chicago at the time when I was beginning to become well known as The Persistent Commoner'.

I am not going to impose upon you a personal account of the difficulties which confront me except to say that I am a victim of what is known as the hereditary system. And the definition of heredity, which you probably know, which I like best of all, is this: if your grandfather didn't have any children, and your father didn't have any children, it is very unlikely that you will have any children. That is the basic problem which confronts me. But one of the nice things about this struggle is the number of kind friends who have written from all over the world to suggest how the problem could be solved.

One man wrote and said, 'Why don't you look at your birth certificate to see if there isn't a misprint, because if you could only prove you were illegitimate, you would be alright.' Of course, bastards cannot inherit titles.

I had a letter from a conservative peer who wasn't on my side, who said as far as he was concerned, I was. The letter that I liked best of all, and that really got nearest the mark was from a friend of mine, an African, who had been with me at the University and is now active in the politics of Uganda. He wrote and said: 'We have been following your struggle with great interest here in Uganda, because in Africa, too, we are fighting against the remnants of witchcraft and tribalism,' and he really touched what the whole thing was about.

Anthony Wedgwood Benn, M.P.

The new Waiter

Here are a couple of stories which can be told at almost any dinner—providing, of course, the right sort of company is present. As for me, I have no shame!

A waiter in a large London hotel thought it was time he had a change, and went to the head waiter at another large well known hotel, and asked if he could give him a job. The head waiter asked him about his previous experience and then said, 'I do not know if you are likely to be quite up to our standards, but we are a little short staffed at the moment and I will give you a trial.'

For his first job, the waiter was given charge of a small dinner party consisting of three men and a very smart girl, wearing a dress with a rather deep neckline. As he was serving the soup to the girl she was leaning across the table talking to one of the men, when part of her anatomy slipped out of the dress and fell into the soup. Showing no concern, the waiter lifted the offending part out of the soup with a spoon, gently cleaning the soup off it, and then replaced it carefully into the top of the dress, again using the spoon.

He thought he had done rather well, and when a suitable moment occurred, he walked across to the head waiter to ask if he had seen the incident, and to enquire what he thought of his treatment of it.

'You did fairly well,' said the head waiter, 'But I'm afraid your standards are not up to what we expect here. You see, *we* always use a *warm* spoon.'

*   *   *

I also like very much, the story of the man who was asked to give an after dinner speech on "Sex". He was duly announced, got to his feet, and said, 'Ladies and Gentlemen . . . it gives me very great pleasure,' and then sat down again!

*　　　*　　　*

I have always remembered the James Agate story of the two waiters meeting by the door of the kitchen, and one whispering to the other, 'He's eaten it.'! ! !

Arthur Askey

Thank you Mrs Green

The most useful story for a speaker I know is a very short and somewhat sentimental one, which can be used when responding to a toast on behalf of the guests. It concerns the small daughter of a friend of mine who was invited to a party. 'When you leave,' said the mother, 'be sure you find Mrs Green and thank her for having you.' At the end of the party, the little girl remembered her instructions, and sought her hostess. 'Mrs Green,' she said, 'thank you so much for having me. *I've been had beautifully.*'

Steve Race

Ending a Speech

I am afraid most of my stories are rather individual, and I have the no doubt insufferably pompous idea that no one could tell them but me! However, the two following concerning the difficulty of *ending* a speech, may be of interest, especially when one is not proposing a toast, and therefore, can't wrench things to a conclusion by suddenly demanding that the company shall be upstanding and drink the confounded toast.

I was speaking to a rather grand theatrical charity dinner in the Grocers' Hall, the last speaker of the evening, and hit on the ingenious device, as I thought, of making great play with my power over the guests—in the sense that it was entirely up to me to make a short speech and let them get to their beds, or a long one and keep them up all night. I said it didn't matter to me: I was staying just round the corner: I could go on for hours: I teased them a bit along these lines, and then said, 'Well, I've decided to do the decent thing. I shall sit down and you can all go home. Goodnight.' I then found there were eight turns on the stage to come, which weren't mentioned on the menu and nobody had thought to to tell me about it.

It's the practice at Eton, once every half, for the Sunday morning speaker to give a peppy sermon, not about God but about the grand old school. One distinguished speaker, with this assignment, had been over-painstaking in devising a dramatic ending. Timed to the second, he ended his peroration thus: 'And, gentlemen, the achievements and triumphs of this great school will continue in the future, as they have in the past, as surely as the school clock will now strike twelve.' Very dramatic. Perfect timing. Two seconds pause, and the clock struck a hundred and twenty-eight.

Basil Boothroyd

A fine Phrase

One of the wisest things I ever heard, and often use, particularly when talking to young people, is a phrase which I once heard used by Vincent Massey, the late Governor General of Canada. He said, addressing a meeting at which I was present: 'You should always be proud of your traditions, but you should never be content with them.'

I was once, truthfully, introduced by a wonderful old coloured Master of Ceremonies at a great dinner in Jamaica, with the words: 'Your Excellency, my Lord Bishop, distinguished guests, ladies and gentlemen, pray for the silence of Sir Edward Leather.'

When the chairman has given a more than usual grandiloquent introduction, I often start by saying, 'Flattery is all right so long as you don't inhale.'

Of the modern school of "so-called" satirists, I sometimes say that they have 'no morals, no manners and dirty finger nails'.

At the end of a more than usually long or serious speech, I sometimes say: 'I now feel like a very small dog at the end of a very long row of trees—I have nothing left to give.'

Ted Leather, M.P.

Saying Grace

Ernie Wise likes this little story.

A mother was entertaining some friends at a dinner party during a heat wave, when she asked her young daughter to say grace.

The daughter looked a little vacant and said: 'But Mother, I don't know what to say.'

'Just say what you heard me say,' said her mother cheerfully.

Obediently the child bowed her head and chanted: 'Oh, Lord, what the heck made me invite this mob when it's 80 in the shade!'

I (Eric Morecambe), like this one.

A little boy had gone to school for the first time, but half way through the morning when his mother was still doing her work, the back door suddenly burst open and the little boy bounded in.

'Whatever are you doing home so early?' asked his mother. 'You should still be in school.'

'Well,' came the reply, 'Henry Jones put his hand up and the teacher said he could go; so I put mine up, and she said I could go, so I've gone, and here I am.'

And here is one we both like.

Two young ladies were having a cycle ride one very hot day when they came to a lake which appeared to be completely hidden, and they decided to risk it and have a quick swim. As one poised, ready for a plunge, minus all her clothing, a man's voice suddenly burst out, 'Sorry miss, this is National Trust land, and no swimming is allowed here.' Making a quick dive into the bracken, the girl shouted,

'Why ever didn't you tell us before we started undressing?'
'There ain't no law, as I know of, against undressing,' came
the reply.

Morecambe and Wise

After Dinner

The dog, considered a sagacious beast,
Does not give tongue when he has had a feast.
Nor does the cow go mooing round the mead
To tell the world that she's enjoyed her feed.
Not even lions, I imagine, roar
After a meal—unless they want some more.
All nature has agreed that it is best,
When fully fed, to ruminate and rest.
The Ancient Romans, flushed with food and wine,
Decided it was wiser to recline.
The cannibal, when he has had his fun,
Does not propose the health of anyone.
But modern man, by some malignant fate,
When he has eaten, simply must orate:
And those who don't, though eager for repose,
Must strain their ears for quantities of prose.
If prose and speeches have effective force,
Our land should be as healthy as a horse.
If wishful drinking rings a magic bell,
Our trade, our industry, should do quite well.
This quaint old custom could be understood
If all the speeches were extremely good.
But it is not a very easy trade:
And more than half of them were best not made.
Oh, what a wise and comfortable thing
If all the toasts were silent—like The King'!
Oh, may I live to hear the Chairman say:
'Friends, you are welcome at our feast today,

Enjoy youselves! Good company—good cheer!
And that's the only speech that you will hear.'

Sir A. P. Herbert

(*Sunday Graphic*—23rd July 1950)

Hospital Humour

As a hospital chaplain, I not infrequently come across amusing incidents which make useful material for including in speeches on suitable occasions.

I once had to pay a visit to the Children's Ward of an Isolation Hospital, and because of the danger of spreading infection, I was asked to wear a white coat.

Said one of the boys: 'Are you a doctor?'

'No,' I replied, 'I'm the padre.'

'You're a daddy then!'

'Well, yes; but my children are mostly grown up—anyhow, that's not why I'm here.'

'Then who are you?'

'I'm a chaplain,' I said.

'Charlie Chaplin?' exclaimed the boy excitedly.

On another occasion, a patient was asked why he was in hospital. The man answered: 'I've colon trouble. They say they are going to take some of it away. Then I suppose I'll be a semi-colon!'

A hospital I visited at one time had a system whereby they placed discs over the beds of the patients indicating to which religious denomination they belonged. The Roman Catholics had a green disc with "R.C" on it; those belonging to the Church of England had a red disc with "C.E." on it; whilst those with Free Church connections had a blue disc with "N.C." on it, standing for Non-conformist.

One day I visited a man in one such bed who had recently undergone a very serious operation. I was surprised to find him extremely perky and evidently well on the way to recovery.

43

'You seem to be doing very well,' I remarked. 'Why do you think you are getting better so quickly?'

'Well,' replied the man, 'I suppose it is because mine was a straightforward case,' and then, pointing to his disc—'*No complications*.' As I walked away from him smiling to myself, I couldn't help thinking that the disc could equally well have stood for '*No Chance*!'

One patient, when giving the usual particulars for his entrance chart, had stated, when asked what his religion was, that he was a "Buddhist". When I read this I decided I would visit the patient, since I was sure that neither the R.C. Priest nor the C. of E. Parson would do so. Reaching the ward, I naturally looked round for a coloured man, but I could not see one. I asked for the help of the Sister, and the man was pointed out to me.

'I understand you are a Buddhist,' I said, as I approached him. 'I have studied comparative religions and thought we might have an interesting talk.'

'A Buddhist?' exclaimed the patient. 'I'm no Buddhist— what do you mean?'

'Well,' I replied, 'that's what your notes say.'

'Oh,' replied the man, 'I remember now. I put that down so that I wouldn't be bothered with any of your lot!'

Hospital Chaplain

44

Wrong Starting Point

Here are three little stories which can be worked into speeches on appropriate occasions.

A car stopped in a country lane and the driver asked an old yokel if he could direct him to the village of Widdlecombe which the motorist knew was not far away.

The yokel scratched his head and thought carefully for a minute or two. Then he said, 'I don't think I can rightly tell you. You see, if I be a-going to Widdlecombe I shouldn't be starting from here.'

*　　　*　　　*

A woman was so delighted with the results she had obtained from some new tablets which she had seen advertised, that she wrote to the manufacturers, saying: 'Since taking your tablets regularly, I am a different woman. My husband is delighted.'

*　　　*　　　*

A commercial traveller who left his car in a "No Parking" area, attached a note to his windscreen which read, 'I must keep this appointment, and I'll lose my job if I don't. *Forgive us our trespasses.*'

When he came back, he found written on the bottom of the note: 'I've been in the Force for twenty years and I'll be sacked if I show any favours. *Lead us not into temptation.*'

Ken Dodd

Troompet Shall Sound

I don't just tell stories on the few occasions when I have to speak. The stuff I use is always very personal. The following is possibly a little too musical for general taste, but then I am a professional singer—and I thought it best to contribute something which is genuine and personal, and full of character.

A young singer once asked me: 'Mr Franklin, what do you think about in "Messiah", when you're not actually singing?' Of course, I had to look professionally shocked at such levity, but, privately, I conceded that he had a point. Between the bass's second aria and his third there is a gap of nearly two hours, and sitting still and with dignity for all that time in full view of the audience, night after night,—you've got problems. What *do* you think about?

Some years ago, there was a principal trumpet of one of the northern orchestras who blatantly and openly put a novel on his music-stand, and read it through all the long hours of rehearsal for "Messiah". He even played the performance from his novel too, for he used to boast that he knew "Messiah" by heart, every single note of it. 'I've played t'Messiah more often than any oother man living,' he once told me. 'I played t'trumpet obligato in "t'Trumpet shall sound" for Santley.' I was astonished. The legendary Sir Charles Santley was born in 1834 and died in 1922, and for more than fifty years was the king of British song. And this man had actually played for Santley—it was like meeting someone who knew Moses!

'Aye,' he said, 'it were fifty-wan yeer ago. I was a boy of thirteen. I'm in my fifty-second season, y'know.' 'Are you indeed?' I said, 'Well, if ever your lip gives, and you have to stop playing, take that big belly of yours up to Covent Garden, and show it to Beecham, and before you know where you are, you'll be on the stage singing "Meister-singer".' 'Nay,' he said, very seriously, 'I do a bit of sing-ging already.' 'Do you?' I said. 'Aye,' he said. 'What sort of thing do you sing?' I asked. 'Well, it depends,' he said, 'I sang "Troompet shall Sound" at smoaking concert last Wednes-day.' 'Oh,' I said. 'And in between vocal phrases, I played troompet obligato,' he said. The vivid picture I had of him on the platform, singing and then having a quick blow, sing-ing and then another quick blow, was almost too much for me, but I managed to say politely, that it must have been very difficult.

'Nay,' he said, arrogantly, and with a contemptuous wave of his arm he swept away the long line of British basses from Charles Santley to Owen Brannigan. 'There's nowt to it. Troompet part's difficult, but there's nowt to t'noomber!'

David Franklin

Heckling Humour

Before the coming of radio and television, the main attractions at any election, were the massed public meetings which were arranged in every constituency. Many people welcomed them as a means of providing fun and excitement, and although there were those who went to listen to the speakers seriously, there were far more who went either to heckle or enjoy the heckling, and the treatment it received from those who were speaking.

Some speakers had the happy knack of being able to give a quick reply, and to make it a devastating one at that. I suppose a master at this sort of thing was the great David Lloyd George, and a reply he once gave to a heckler during an address on Home Rule for Ireland, is still remembered today. With typical Welsh fervour, L.G. was saying: 'I not only believe in Home Rule for Ireland, but also for Scotland, and for Wales...' From the back of the hall came a loud shout: 'To hell with Home Rule.' Without a moment's hesitation, the great man turned on the heckler and snapped back: 'That's right, every man for his own country: I admire a loyalist.'

On another occasion, when the Welsh wizard was speaking, a persistent heckler kept shouting: 'What we need is a change of Government.' Finally, Lloyd George looked down at him and said: 'What *you* want, my friend, is a change of drink.'

Sir Winston Churchill was another who was good at dealing with hecklers. At one of his meetings, a man was reported to have shouted to him: 'If you was the ruddy member for Heaven, I wouldn't vote for you.' Sir Winston chose his words carefully and then replied slowly: 'Indeed! If I ever have the honour of representing that celestial constituency—which is unlikely— I am quite sure your name will not be on the electoral roll.'

On another occasion, a heckler kept shouting the one word 'Rot' whilst Sir Winston was speaking, and when he had shouted this a number of times, Sir Winston paused and said: 'I am bound to say, Sir, that you are being very frank. You have told us several times exactly what is in your mind. I hope you have cleared it all out by now.'

Until comparatively recently, election meetings held at street corners were quite common. On one occasion, a candidate was declaring the policy of his party with great fervour, when someone in the audience suddenly hurled a cabbage at him. The missile missed his head by only a few inches and fell behind him. Breaking off his speech, he stepped from his platform and picked up the offending weapon. Returning to his platform, he held the cabbage in his hand above his head and said: 'Excuse me, I think one of you has lost his head. Would you like it back?' When the laughter had died down, he was allowed to finish his speech uninterrupted.

One very well known story is of the speaker who was suddenly asked: 'If returned, will you support the abolition of the Decalogue?' 'Certainly,' answered the candidate promptly, 'I am all in favour of doing just that.' During the roar of laughter which followed, the candidate turned to his agent and whispered: 'Good gracious, what have I done now?' 'You've only promised to abolish the Ten Commandments,' the agent told him.

Jack Norman

49

The Porter's Assessment

It is not easy to think of funny stories just off the cuff, but here are two which I think are amusing and which can often prove useful.

The first is reputed to have emanated from a well known Public School. The second master entering the Hall one day on his way to the headmaster's study, observed some ladies being shown into the waiting room by the school porter. 'Who are those ladies waiting to see the headmaster?' he asked, when the porter reappeared. 'Ladies, sir?' the porter replied, 'them's not ladies, them's parents!'

The second concerns a psychologist and his friend who were deep in argument at a window overlooking a street in which excavating work was being done by navvies. Suddenly the psychologist exclaimed: 'Remarkable! You see a dozen men below with barrows—eleven push them, and the twelfth pull his. Now why—there must be some explanation—possibly some deep-seated urge—some inhibition—some . . . but let's go and talk to him.'

Down to the street they went and called the man over. 'We have observed,' the psychologist began, 'That, whereas your comrades on this work push their barrows before them, you pull yours behind you, and we feel sure there is some fundamental reason for this. Would you care to help us to discover it by saying why you do so?'

'Blimey gov'nor,' the navvy replied, 'I 'ates the sight of the damn'd thing!'

Jack Longland

Poor Mr Swaffer

After the first night of Noel Coward's very fine play *The Vortex*, in which Coward himself brilliantly played the lead, Hannen Swaffer, Lord of the Popular Journalists, saw him after the play.

'Coward,' he said. 'You act better than you write.'

The reply was instantaneous.

'So do you, Mr Swaffer.'

Stephen Potter

Just a Little Change

I have always remembered, with amusement, a story which I heard shortly after the end of the War. If you are telling it, you have to choose your audience carefully, and it is, of course, quite untrue.

It relates to the attention given to Canterbury by German aircraft, and particularly to the damage suffered by the Cathedral. A special fund was launched to cover the repairs, and the Archbishop was highly pleased when he received a message from a group of important American businessmen telling him they would like to meet him and discuss certain terms under which they would be willing to donate a million dollars to the fund.

The Archbishop arranged a meeting and thought it advisable to ask as many bishops as possible to be present for such an important occasion. The Americans duly arrived but thought it would be better not to discuss their proposition with all the bishops in attendance. They preferred, they said, to talk to the Archbishop alone first.

The bishops, all expectant and excited, waited outside whilst the discussion between the Archbishop and the Americans, went on. At length the Archbishop came out. The bishops crowded round him and asked feverishly: 'What is it? What is it? What do they want for this handsome gift of a million dollars?'

'They want me to change two or three words in the Lord's Prayer, but I do not feel that I can do it.'

'But, surely,' said one of the bishops, 'the changing of two or three words, for the sake of a million dollars would not be all that important. What exactly do they want you to do?'

'Well,' said the Archbishop, 'they are trying to persuade me to change the words "Give us this day our daily bread" into "Give us this day our so-and-so corn flakes".'

*   *   *

A Welsh preacher waxed vehement on one occasion and said to his congregation: 'I want to speak to you about phenomena that occur in nature, but I expect many of you do not even know what a phenomenon is. Let me try to explain. If you were out in the country and saw a cow lying on the grass, that would not be a phenomenon; it would merely be one of the cow's natural habits. If you heard the song of a bird up in the air as it flitted from tree to tree, that would not be a phenomenon; that, too, would be a part of its natural habits. If you came across a field and saw growing there a tall and handsome thistle, that would not be a phenomenon. It might be a bit of a nuisance to the farmer, but it would nevertheless be a part of nature which you could accept. But my friends, if you were to go for a walk on a Sunday morning and see a cow in a field, sitting on a thistle, and singing like a lark, then *that* would be a phenomenon indeed.'

*   *   *

What I have always considered was the best example of quick-thinking I have ever experienced, occurred at a dinner party at which I was present when I was serving in the Seychelle Islands. It was a large party, held around Christ-

53

mas time, with all the important people in the island present. It came to the time for serving the turkey, which had been specially flown in, live, from Kenya for the occasion, as turkeys did not flourish in the Seychelles. It was thus the *only* turkey on the island. A servant entered the door with a magnificent silver dish bearing 'the' turkey with all the usual trimmings round it. As he entered the room, he tripped and dropped the dish and all its contents on the floor. As he stooped to pick them up, the hostess, quick as a flash, turned to him and said: 'No, Louis, I did not want *that* turkey; go back and fetch the other one.'

Michael Hunt
(*Anglia Television's Weather Man*)

Something She didn't Do!

There are two stories I would mention—the first that of Lord Robert Cecil who was Bishop of Exeter and very vague. At a dinner he was attending, wine was poured for all the guests save for an old lady on his left, who was given water. When she plucked up courage later in the meal to ask if she could be given wine, he said, 'I'm sorry, I thought you were a member of the "Temperance League".' 'Oh, no,' she replied, 'the "Purity League".' 'Oh, yes,' he replied, 'I knew there was something you didn't do.'

The second one relates to the late Marquess of Reading (the second) who, as an undergraduate, was asked during Sir Roland Twyford's Lord Mayoralty, to address a dinner attended amongst others by Lady Oxford. He horrified the assembled company by saying that when invited to propose the health of the Lord Mayor of London he would have thought that some care would have been taken to see that he was seated in order of precedence. He then went on to say that he had lived for 25 years on the Great Western Railway and knew that it was Twyford, Reading, Oxford, and not Reading, Oxford, Twyford. Relief all round!

Jeremy Thorpe, M.P.

A Bonny Baby

This is one of my favourite after-dinner stories.

Two men had been dining together at their club and had gone on talking, after a great deal to drink, so that by the time they got round to the subject of the weight of newly-born babies, they were definitely fuddled.

First man: 'D'you know, ol' boy, when I was born, I only weighed four and a half pounds.

Second man: 'Good Lord! Did you live?'

First man: 'Did I live? You ought to see me now.'

J. B. Priestley, M.A. Ll.D.

My Biggest Blunder

I once arrived to address an election meeting, where I was the candidate, at the end of a long and very tiring day. In a packed and, on the whole, sympathetic hall, two people, a middle-aged man and woman, sitting together, persistently interrupted me. After about twenty minutes my temper frayed, and when the man shouted out some insulting remark, I snapped back at him, 'Be quiet sir, or I'll have you put out.' Then, seeing that the woman was about to add something further, I added 'and that goes for your wife too.' At that moment I realized that I had no reason to suppose that they were man and wife or indeed anything to do with one another, except that they happened to be sitting together. Knowing that tiredness had made me behave rudely, I tried to put matters right—genuinely. 'If,' I said, 'she is your wife.'

That is certainly the biggest blunder that I can ever recall making in public.

John Freeman, M.B.E.

I only needed a Bottle of Perfume

A few years ago I was filming in Paris. An old friend of mine had asked me to bring him back a bottle of toilet water from a very distinguished shop in the Faubourg St-Honore. I walked down the Faubourg a couple of times to case the joint. Frankly, I was terrified. The store was staffed by very elegant, sophisticated young women, and my French was negligible.

However, I couldn't let my friend down so I plucked up courage and entered. I selected the least sophisticated young woman that I could see and murmured something about 'desiring some eau do toilette'. Being an actor, I suppose I must have accentuated the final word of the sentence.

The young lady gave me an almost motherly glance, and went to converse with a slightly more elderly young woman who stared at me and then nodded.

My young woman then took an enormous, mediaeval key from a hook and beckoned me to follow. We descended to a basement stock room and then continued to a further stock-room. This rather surprised me as the upstairs showrooms were loaded with the very commodity I was seeking. We traversed a third stockroom even deeper in the dungeon. 'Adventure?' I wondered. 'Perhaps she's leading me to her lair?'

Then she struck the key into a miserable little door labelled W.C. and said, 'Voila, M'sieur. La toilette!'

I feel confident that the laughter which exploded in that highly sophisticated emporium when I explained that there had been a mistake, could have been heard on the second floor of the Eiffel Tower.

A few years ago I was a guest at a dinner at the Savoy Hotel given by "E" Division of the Metropolitan Police.

The moment came when the Toastmaster announced: 'Your President and his Lady wish to take wine with Superintendent Lockhart.' This, I am happy to say, aroused a certain amount of applause. After I had sat down, a very famous Chief-Superintendent, who had recently retired from the Flying Squad (and who did not watch TV), turned to my host and said, 'Who is this fellow Lockhart?'

My host replied with a smile, 'Oh, he's doing rather well. He solves a major crime at least once a week.'

'Never heard of him,' said the ex-detective. 'He must be a provincial superintendent!'

*   *   *

A story was related at a similar function (which I am sure is not original) of a Police Officer who resigned to seek solitude in a Monastery.

'You're welcome, my son,' said the Abbott, 'but you realize here we observe a vow of silence. You must not speak without permission.' This was just what the ex-policeman wanted.

After three years he applied for an interview. 'Permission to speak, my son,' said the Abbott.

'Father, could I have a little more sugar in my tea?' asked the ex-policeman.

'I think that could be arranged,' said the Abbott.

Five years later another interview was sought. 'Father, could I have more porridge for my breakfast?'

The Abbott sighed. 'I will see what I can do, my son.'

Six years later, a third interview was sought. 'Father, I don't seem to be settling down here. I have decided to return to the outside world.'

'I should jolly well think so,' said the Abbott. 'You've done nothing but complain ever since you came here!'

Raymond Francis

You Must be Discreet

It is said that if you pop a dinner into the mouth of a politician up will come a speech. You must be careful, however, not to pop a speech into the mouths of some politicians or otherwise up will come your dinner!'

John Hall, O.B.E., M.P.

Saying Grace

Whenever I have to attend a public dinner or luncheon, and the Chairman—or more usually, some visiting cleric—rises to say Grace, I am reminded of the first time I ever heard Grace said at a meal. I'm afraid, although I was brought up on the Scottish Borders, we were a somewhat heathen lot; we just got down to it the moment the soup arrived, with never a thought for the Almighty.

I was at boarding-school in Edinburgh, and we were only allowed out for lunch on Sunday if vouched for, collected by, and returned safely by some bona-fide relations. By halfway through my first term, I had gone through all the branches of the family tree known to me . . . and, to be honest, they had had their fill of me. I had quite an appetite in those days. I was forced, therefore, to explore the lesser-known twigs of the tree, and to my delight I found some third cousins, twice removed, who lived within hailing distance of the school and who were in due course dragooned into inviting me out to Sunday lunch. It was, I remember, a large and lovely Georgian house on the outskirts of Edinburgh, and after the formality of introductions to unknown aunts and uncles and cousins were over, we were ushered—to my relief—into an enormous dining-room. There were eight of us, and the maid—in stiffly starched apron and cap—arrived bearing a colossal tureen of Scotch broth as the first course.

It was the *real* Scotch broth: so stiff and so thick that the spoon almost stood up in it. It was served in soup plates of a most sensible size and depth, and Willow pattern design. I was, as always, starving; the moment my plate was filled and put in front of me, I dived in from the deep end. I was well through the broth, and wondering about second helpings, when I realized, that apart from the noise of my soup-intake, a solemn hush had descended round the table. I looked up and to my horror, saw that all heads were bowed and not a soup-spoon, save my own, had been touched. There was a pregnant pause, and then my uncle (if he *was* my uncle: at any rate the very hirsute old gentleman at the head of the table) said in a glorious Scots bass-baritone: 'For what we are about to receive, and for what Alan has alrrready received, may the Lorrd mak' us trrruly thankful.'

It quite put me off the rest of the meal; I was only able to eat three helpings of the silverside and dumplings.

Alan Melville

The Endless Speech

Two after-dinner speeches I have liked, are these:

A certain Peer had a dream, during which he dreamt that he was making a speech. It seemed to him that he had been embarked for a very long time on a pointless, endless, stream of discord which he was addressing to the House of Lords. The speech just went on and on and on. Then, in a flash, the Peer awoke—and found he *was* addressing the House of Lords.

*　　*　　*

The second story concerns a report which appeared in a local weekly. The report read: 'We regret that in last week's edition there appeared the statement that Detective Robinson has retired from the *Defective* Police Force. This, of course, was an error and should have read Detective Robinson has retired from the Detective Police *Farce*.'

Sir Ralph Richardson

Population Problems

These three little stories are all useful for differing occasions.

A lecturer who was holding forth on the serious population increase, said: 'Do you realize that somewhere in the world a woman is giving birth to a child every minute, day and night. What are we going to do about it?'

A woman at the back of the hall piped up: 'I think the *first* thing to do is to find *that* woman and stop her.'

*　　*　　*

The Principal Surgeon, addressing a body of students, said: 'In view of the fact that electricity has an inflammatory effect upon silk, I think we must take another look at the underclothing of those nurses who work in the "Theatre".'

*　　*　　*

In connection with the appalling total of road accidents, a Cardiff magistrate once commented: 'One motorist thinks there is nothing about and meets another motorist who also thinks there is nothing about. Then, there is often an accident, and at least one of them is definitely no longer about.'

A. A. Payne

Whisky for the Judge

To illustrate the incorruptibility of British public life, I have often related this story:

An American who had established a business here, ran into a spot of trouble, and he went to his closest English friend for advice. 'Frank,' he said, 'I have a dissatisfied customer who threatens to take me to Court. The trouble is that I think he has got a good case. How would it help if I slipped the Judge a bottle of whisky?' Frank replied with the utmost horror: 'My dear Joe, you just can't do that sort of thing in England. If anything, under British Justice, the whisky would make the Judge rule against you, even if you had a good case, which you say you haven't, so don't take the risk.'

Two weeks later the case came up for hearing, and much to the Englishman's surprise, his American friend won his case. Intrigued, he 'phoned him up. 'Joe,' he said, 'how did you manage to get off when you hadn't a leg to stand on?' 'Well,' replied the American, 'it was simple. I bore in mind what you said about British justice, so I sent the Judge a crate of whisky and I put the other guy's name on it!'

Geoffrey Johnson-Smith, M.P.

Eliza the tit-bit

These two little stories I have often found worth telling.

A little girl in Sunday School was told the story of Elijah the Tishbite. She went home and said, 'Oh, Mummy, we had a lovely story today and I can remember it word for word.' Mother said, 'Tell me dear.' So the little girl said, 'Eliza appeared before the King wrapped in a camel's hair, and said, "Behold, O King, I am Eliza the Tit-bit".'

* * *

He was an Etonian who failed in his scripture examination and complained bitterly. He said, 'After all, Sir, how could I be expected to know that Dan and Beersheba were *places*? I thought they were man and wife like Sodom and Gomorrah.'!!!

C. A. Joyce

Anglo-American Relations

I generally find that the following comes in handy when talking about Anglo-American relations, especially when there are Americans present:

'The world today is divided into two camps; those who thank God that the Pilgrim Fathers landed on the Plymouth Rock; and those others who wish to God that the Plymouth Rock had landed on the Pilgrim Fathers.'

Ludovic Kennedy

Reflections of a Screenwriter

We are all familiar with the Hollywood legend, but we screenwriters tend to view all this hoo-hah with some degree of scepticism. What really upsets us is the fact that in the world of film-making, the writer is the forgotten man. He is like the soldier: loved by everybody when there is a crisis, forgotten and ignored when the crisis is over. If you read the publicity handouts and reviews once a film has been made, you seldom see the name of the man who wrote the screenplay. I suppose the general public is expected to believe that the stars and the director and the producer, whose names are in such big print, made up the words as they went along.

Of course, many films *do* look as though they were improvised, which is something that even a screenwriter will admit in his less testy moments (for example, after he has eaten a meal, or paid the last instalment on the account of his children's shoes).

But the trouble here is that everybody fancies himself as a writer. The chief hazard of a writer's life is the woman who bears down upon him at a party, a shining light in her eyes and a manuscript in her hands, and who then proceeds to bore the hell out of him. She is a great and talented writer, of course, but she just cannot get recognition. If only you would look over the MSS, perhaps collaborate with her, even put your name under hers on the script, etc, etc.

A dentist once took advantage of the fact that I was lying in the chair, watching his electric drill with a wary eye, to tell me that he had always had a hankering to be a writer. He had, he said, a hundred stories in his head which only required to be put down on paper. Encouraged by my silence (I had a thick chunk of cotton wool wedged in my mouth), he went on to suggest that he should tell me the stories, I would write them down, and we should market them under our joint names and split the proceeds fifty-fifty. In this arrangement, it was quite clear that he considered my role to be that of the general labourer.

When I emerged from this ordeal, I made a counter-offer. I suggested that he should put my name with his own on the brass plate outside the surgery door, and allow me to come in and fill a few cavities after he had drilled the teeth. He was quite annoyed by my levity. Apparently he thought that his professional skill was something sacred, while mine was something that could be picked up in a couple of minutes.

However, most screenwriters learn not to be too sensitive. It can take years and be painful, but the lesson sinks in. We become used to listening to advice from the stars, the feature players, the director, the cameraman, the publicity officer, the tea-boy and the chief executive's mistress. And over our Irish tea at various screenwriter gatherings, we pass the purple hearts and tell each other, with wry smiles, of the latest antics of those teeming thousands of people who have taken unto themselves, without reason, meaning or experience, the unofficial title of script consultant. It was at one of these fiestas that I heard the following story.

It concerns a man whom I shall call Zoob, partly to protect the innocent and partly because it is a name with only four letters, and I can write it quicker. Zoob was an assistant-deputy-cost-accountant at one of the bigger studios and his main job was to go through the scripts and make out an estimate of what it would cost to turn them into the finished film.

It wasn't a very important job, but Zoob thought it was, and here we must forgive him. Every man should take pride in his work, and in any case, Zoob had an additional reason for his feeling of self-importance. Some years before, when he was a mere costing-clerk, he had been called upon to make a provisional budget for an adventure drama about Robin Hood. He had read the script very carefully, and it had occurred to him that it would be possible, in one scene, to cut down the number of extras required at an elaborate banquet. His suggestion had been followed, despite the protests of the writer, and what had been an enormous bean-feast in the castle hall, became an intimate dinner party in the Sheriff's bedroom, and just the Sheriff and Maid Marian in attendance. This Zoob had managed to combine sex with economy and shown, in one superb flash of brilliance, that he understood the fundamental ethic on which film-making is based.

Zoob had never forgotten this experience. It was his greatest triumph. As the years went on he read other scripts and made other suggestions, some of which were adopted but nothing ever quite equalled this first major break-through. In private, to his wife and his friends, Zoob adopted the casual pose of a man who was in at the very heart of film-making; he dropped names like Sophia and Spencer and Garbo and Sam and Darryl like ripe plums into almost every conversation. It was generally accepted that his was the brain that shaped scripts and mobilised resources for our biggest and most successful productions. Zoob, to do him justice, did not actively assert that this was the case, but on the other hand, he did not deny it either. He would merely smile mysteriously, which in some circles is often regarded as the hall mark of wisdom.

He was now about 45, a short man, running to fat. He had a rowing machine and he ate only natural food, grown without artificial chemicals, but he could not quite shake off the slight bulge which stretched his waistcoat. He travelled by train, walking from home to the station, and from the station to the studio, all in the cause of exercise. At lunch time he avoided the studio restaurant, except when important stars were dining there, and he would buy fruit from a stall nearby and eat this as he walked. He was, as I hope I have established, a very sincere and dedicated man.

The owner of the fruit and vegetable stall, whom I shall call Fred (which is another four letter word), knew Mr Zoob of course, and referred to him as a man of influence and power in the studios, and on one particular day he pointed to a new sign which was hung across the top of his stall and asked, respectfully:

'I'd very much appreciate your candid opinion of my new sign, Mr Zoob.'

Mr Zoob looked up. He put on his spectacles and read the sign. It said:

FRESH FRUIT SOLD HERE TODAY

'Just thought it might brighten up the old stall,' said Fred apprehensively, for Zoob was taking his time to comment.

'Yes, indeed,' said Zoob, 'an excellent sign. First rate.'

'You like it?' asked Fred, smiling.

'Well,' said Zoob, 'you did ask for my candid opinion. I've got some experience in this sort of thing, as you know, Fred. It does provide a very good basis.'

'Basis?' said Fred.

'It just needs a little work on it,' said Zoob. 'Now let me see. It's too long. That's the fault. Needs to be crisp, taut. Essence of a good script. I should take out the first word.'

'The first word?'

'Yes. Fresh—it has the wrong psychological approach. It can set up the suggestion in the mind of the customer that perhaps your fruit isn't always fresh, that yesterday it wasn't fresh if you follow me. Definitely wrong.'

'I think you're right Mr Zoob,' said Fred, and he stood on a box and pinned a piece of paper over the offending word. 'Now,' he said, 'how is that?'

'Still not right,' he murmured. 'Do you know, I think you could dispense with the last word. It carries no value. The public know that you are selling the fruit today. It's a matter of common-sense. Cover it up.'

Fred covered it up. Still Mr Zoob remained unsatisfied.

'I don't think you need the word "here" either, Fred. You are not selling your wares in Whitehall or Wapping. We know you are here. It's superfluous. Weakens the whole thing.'

Fred covered up the word "here". Still Zoob considered the sign. The pause was a little longer.

'Got it!' he cried. 'Sold—that is quite wrong, Fred. It will alienate the public. They know that you are not going to give the fruit away. They know they will have to buy it. On the other hand, it is bad psychology to remind them of the fact that they will have to spend money.'

Fred covered up this word also. Now all that remained was the solitary word "FRUIT". Mr Zoob smiled.

'Perfect,' he said. 'Short, sharp, to the point.'

And with a smile at Fred, he walked away. Fred looked up at the sign. It seemed rather pathetic—the word "FRUIT"—and the bits of paper sticking to it.

Just then, one of his customers, a woman, came up to the stall. She was just an ordinary member of the public, with no particular experience with signs or scripts, certainly not in the same street as Mr Zoob in this respect. In fact, she had never been inside a studio in her entire life, which indicates the depth of her ignorance.

'Oh, I don't like that, Fred,' she said, looking up at the sign. 'It's a mess.'

Fred took down the bits of paper and let her see the whole sign.

'That's lovely,' she beamed, smiling. 'Really lovely.' And she spent at least a fiver at the stall, on tomatoes, lettuces and apples, and bananas and oranges.

Fred did not put the paper back, or alter the sign because, after all, the customer is always right. And Mr Zoob did not notice the sign again anyway, because he was far too busy trying to work out in his mind how he could eliminate 200 Vikings from a projected film and save the studio some thousands of pounds. And somewhere, buried in all this, there is a moral, but at the moment I can't think what it could be.

Lord Willis

Growing Orchids

A gardening story I sometimes use is the one about a poor old gardener who had to have an operation. Back in his bed, when it was all over, he opened his eyes and saw the doctor standing there. 'Doctor,' he said, in a quivering voice, 'am I going to get better?'

'Yes,' said the doctor, 'you are going to be quite alright.'

A little later the old gardener opened his eyes again, and once more the doctor was standing looking at him. 'Doctor,' he asked, 'am I still going to be able to do my garden?'

The doctor reassured him that he was going to be quite alright and told him there was no reason why he should not be able to do all his gardening as usual. After a minute or two's reflection the patient looked up at the doctor again and asked, 'Doctor, will I be able to grow orchids?'

The doctor touched him gently on the arm and very reassuringly said, 'Yes, of course, you will be able to grow orchids.'

There was a moment's pause and then the patient said, 'That must have been a mighty wonderful operation, doctor, —'cos I could never grow orchids before.'

Percy Thrower
N.D. Hort., F.Inst. P.A., F.R.H.S.

Drinking Bouts

Here are three amusing stories which are suitable for many occasions:

The first concerns Sir Winston Churchill and my work in the House of Commons. One day a group of us had an all night sitting and we were having our eggs and bacon in the Members' Dining Room at about 3 a.m. when we were joined by Sir Winston Churchill who was then Prime Minister. He sat at the same table but paid no interest in our conversation. We continued our conversation which was about a certain well known Member of Parliament who seemed to be taking a little more alcoholic refreshment than was strictly needed before making a speech. Someone volunteered the information that these drinking bouts were getting more frequent. At this, Sir Winston raised his head and demanded, 'What is this about drinking bouts?' One of us repeated what we had been saying, to which Sir Winston replied that he was very sorry indeed to hear about this particular man having drinking bouts. 'That is bad,' he said, 'you should never have drinking bouts. You should be like me—drink deeply but consistently.'

The next story is of a different nature but is an excellent example, I think, of a brilliant repartee. One day I was dining with a famous hostess who married a man to whom she had been a secretary and who was many years older than she. At dinner the conversation turned on the subject of an ex-diplomat who, having retired from the service, had just married for the first time a girl some twenty or thirty years his junior who had been his secretary. At the dinner party was a young diplomat who, without thinking, said,

'Any man who marries a girl where the difference of age is so great must be a fool, but if she was his secretary then he must be doubly a fool.' A hush fell on the dinner party. Our hostess came to the rescue and said, 'Young man, that comes ill from someone dining at my table,' because this was precisely what she had done herself. We all concentrated on our food. The position, however, was saved when the young diplomat said, 'I realize that, Lady .... but I am not dining at your table, I fell through the floor five seconds ago.

There was general laughter including the hostess and the situation was completely saved.

Children are often unpredictable. With my children at the table my wife and I were discussing a business acquaintance and his wife at dinner the day before he and his wife were coming to lunch. The couple arrived a little early and my young son aged 6 was the only person in the hall when they arrived. He proudly showed them into the drawing room where my wife was, announcing in a piping voice, 'Here are the .... mama, and they don't look stinking rich.' You can imagine the embarrassment this caused.

Sir John Rodgers, Bart., M.P.

Second Prize

Here are one or two stories which I think dear old "Colonel Chinstrap" might have told at Regimental Dinners—always providing, of course, that he had been asked to speak, and was capable, at the time, of doing so!

A stranger was staying at a country inn for the night, and when he arrived he found a private party was going on. Although he was longing to get some rest, he was dragged into the party for a few hours, and during this time he purchased a ticket for a raffle which was being held.

Eventually he managed to break away from the party and go up to his room, but before he could finally settle down, he heard a loud thumping at his door and a man was shouting: 'You'll have to come down for a little while. You've won the second prize in the draw.'

He walked sleepily to the door and enquired what he had won.

'You can kiss and cuddle the barmaid for half an hour,' came the reply.

'Good gracious! If that is the second prize, whatever is the first?'

'Two pound fifty!'

*   *   *

A kangaroo walked into a public house and asked the barman to pour him out a whisky. As the barman did this the kangaroo placed a paw into his pouch and pulled out a ten pound note. The barman took this and gave the kangaroo one five pound note in change. The kangaroo placed the note in his pouch, finished his drink, and walked towards the door.

As he was going out the barman shouted: 'Good morning. I've never had the pleasure of serving a kangaroo before; I hope you will come in again.'

'Not likely,' said the kangaroo. 'With Scotch at £5 a glass!'

*   *   *

A customer went into his "local" one evening, walked briskly across to the landlord and asked: 'Can you remember how much I spent in here last night?'

'Not really,' said the landlord, 'but I do remember you were in for quite a while and that you paid for a number of rounds.'

'Do you remember if I changed four fivers?'

The landlord thought for a moment and then said: 'Yes, I think I can remember your changing a fiver on four occasions.'

'Thank goodness for that,' said the customer, heaving a big sigh of relief. *'I thought I'd lost them!'*

Jack Train

John's Garden

This story is useful if you have been asked to open a Garden Party or Horticultural Show.

John Smith bought one of those old cottages in the country. It had been unoccupied for some time and the garden in particular had been badly neglected.

But John was a keen gardener. He worked hard, and in the following summer he had a beautiful garden that was much admired by locals and visitors alike.

One evening, as John stood by his garden gate, smoking his pipe, the Vicar came along. He greeted John and as his mind and eye tried to cope with the splendour of the flower beds, he commented: 'Mr Smith, isn't the work of the Lord truly wonderful?'

'Maybe so,' replied John, 'but you should have seen it when He had it to Himself.'

The following story always seems to go down well at a wedding reception.

In the weeks preceding her wedding, the young bride was getting increasingly excited. She made several visits to the Manse to consult the Minister about the marriage ceremony. Restraining his exasperation, he explained it all again slowly, asking her to bear in mind particularly the sequence of the ceremony and everything would fall into place. Arriving at the church, she would walk up the AISLE on her father's arm. The groom and best man would be already in their place before the ALTAR. When she reached them she would take her place alongside the groom and her father would join her mother at the front of the church. The Minister would then ask the congregation to join in singing a HYMN, after which he would proceed with the ceremony and all she need do was to repeat certain words after him.

The poor girl tried very hard to absorb it all and finally agreed that she had the sequence firmly in mind.

And she had! On the great day as she walked up the aisle, the Minister wondered at the look of consternation on the faces of the congregation, until she came close enough for him to hear the words she was speaking to herself quietly but with great determination. They were 'AISLE ALTAR HYMN.' 'I'll alter him!'

Tom Fraser, M.P.

Soldier's Receipt

My only reaction to dinners is a sinking feeling in the pit of my stomach amounting almost to nausea at the thought of having to speak for my dinner later on! As a matter of fact I rarely go to these sort of affairs if I can help it because I find them torture.

Two stories which come from the War, and which may be of interest, are the following.

Into one of the Prisoner-of-War camps came a very angry German who said he had been the Paymaster of his Unit and, when he had been captured, he was in the possession of DM40,000. These had been removed from him by a British private soldier. He demanded their return as such a practice was contrary to the usages of war. He then added, 'I made the soldier give me a receipt.' The interrogating officer said, 'Show me it,' whereupon he produced from his pocket a dirty bit of paper on which was written: 'This bastard *had* DM40,000, now he hasn't'! This was a typical piece of soldier's wit.

During the War, the Germans, as you know, formed many camps of workers from the territories which they occupied, displaced persons' camps as they were known. When the War was over, these people started breaking out of their camps and beating up the Germans—a very natural reaction, but unfortunately by now we were responsible for law and order and had to prevent these things happening. We therefore had to place a certain number of soldiers in each camp and into one particular camp consisting of 1,000 displaced persons from many different countries, all we could put was one Lance Corporal and 10 men, as we were very short of men at that time. As the Company Commander said 'It is the best we can do—if you get into trouble, let me know and I will try to help.'

The Corporal was a very unusual young man. The first thing he did was to hold elections and got himself elected Head of the camp—a good start. He then realized that the children were running wild, so he found teachers and got schools going. The displaced persons had been living all "higgledy-piggledy" and he decided to sort them out, so he sent for the elders of the Camp and said, 'It seems to me that a lot of you ought to get married.' They agreed that this was the case, so he added, 'Well, you can count on me,' and he married seventeen couples in six weeks.

The Camp was completely peaceful from then on.

Lt. Gen. Sir Brian Horrocks,
K.C.B., K.B.E., D.S.O., M.C.

Meeting Uproar

It was a very noisy meeting; he was a very dull speaker. But he was persistent. Through all the disturbances in the body of the hall he went monotonously on. His audience became more and more restless and, after a time, began arguing among themselves, then shouting and finally fighting. Through the uproar the speaker droned on. A great fight began in the far corner of the hall. After a while a huge Irishman rose from the struggling throng brandishing aloft the wriggling body of another man. He was just about to dash it to the floor when a voice called out from the other corner, 'Don't waste 'im Paddy, kill the speaker wid 'im.'

Sir Kenneth Thompson, Bart., M.P.

Australian Emigrant

Here are a couple of stories which I find useful on suitable occasions.

An Australian decided to emigrate to England. Some miles out from Southampton the ship sank. He was left paddling for the shore on a raft when a pigeon came overhead and asked him if he would like a tow. He was willing to try anything once, and so he threw up a nylon rope which was then attached to the pigeon which flapped its way to Southampton, bringing along the Australian with his raft.

Into Port, the Australian reported to the Immigration Authorities, who asked him how he got there and what he wanted.

He said he had come for a job. 'What are you?' asked the Immigration Officer. 'A ballet dancer,' said the Australian. 'So sorry,' came the answer, 'we don't have any jobs for pigeon-toed ballet dancers.'

*　　　*　　　*

Two Civil Servants and an M.P. in a car were lost in a remote village in Wales.

They asked a local where they were. They got what they thought was a brisk reply: 'You are lost in a car, in fog, in Wales.'

They discussed the matter, and the M.P. made the point that this was a perfect Parliamentary Answer. 'It's short: it's accurate: it reveals nothing and it asks for a Supplementary!'

Kenneth Lewis, M.P.

Changing a Note

A man met his friend whom he had not seen for some time and asked him how he was getting on.

'I'm making money,' the friend replied.

'Making money?'

'Yes,' said the friend, 'I've just made this £18 note.'

'An £18 note? What do you expect to do with that?'

'Oh,' said his friend, 'I'll take it across to Ireland. They'll take it, you see.'

The next time the man met his friend, he asked him how he had got on.

'Oh,' said the friend, 'I just took it into a pub and asked the barman if he'd change an £18 note for me. "Sure," he says, "and how would you like it, two nines or six threes?"

Eamonn Andrews

On the Air

On the "Today" programme from time to time we get some pretty silly assignments. Quite often just to fill in time I broadcast a piece of useless information, and one morning I happened to say that the record jump for a porpoise was 16 feet. Not long after making this remark, the public relations officer for a well known airline telephoned me and said that I was quite wrong. He knew of a porpoise that had jumped 20 feet every day of its life 5 times a day, and would I like to meet it? I replied, 'I suppose it's in Miami.' 'Yes,' he said.

I agreed to go and meet this porpoise on one condition, which was that I should fly out to Miami over the weekend and be back for the programme on Monday morning, so that I could close the programme on the Friday morning by saying, 'Goodbye. I hope you have a nice weekend. I am going to Miami for the weekend to interview a porpoise and will be back on Monday.'

After a couple of hours' delay I left London Airport at 2.00 on a Boeing 707 and arrived in Miami two hours late. As you know, in the tropics the sun goes down very quickly, and everybody was very worried about whether I would have time to meet the porpoise before it got dark. They were so anxious they arranged for a helicopter to fly me from the airport to the Seaquarium and a police car was laid on to take me back.

When I got there I found my recording machine was broken. I had only ten minutes with the porpoise and had no story to bring back to London, so in desperation I asked the managing director of the Seaquarium if he had any tapes. He gave me a couple and I returned to London.

Surely it would have been much easier if he had put them in the post originally!

Jack de Manio

Index